Original title:
Lavender Lyrics

Copyright © 2025 Creative Arts Management OÜ
All rights reserved.

Author: Simon Fairchild
ISBN HARDBACK: 978-1-80566-662-2
ISBN PAPERBACK: 978-1-80566-947-0

Spray of Violet Mist

In a garden so bright, a sprayer does dance,
The flowers all giggle at its silly prance.
With a twist and a turn, it sends out a spray,
Plants laugh at the sight, 'What a glorious play!'

A bee in a top hat buzzes with glee,
Sipping nectar cocktails, it dances with spree.
The butterflies chuckle, they join in the show,
As petals all whirl in a violet flow.

Moments Cradled in Purple

In a cup made of clouds, a sip of delight,
Sipping sweet tea that twinkles just right.
Cookies like crowns sit atop of a throne,
In this land of purple, we're never alone.

The squirrels tell jokes, with berries as snacks,
While giggling blooms wear their funniest hats.
Time skips on rainbows, we bounce with a cheer,
In moments of purple, nothing's austere.

Gentle Secrets of the Twilight

As the stars start to wink, the shadows will play,
Whispers of mischief in twilight's bouquet.
A frog in a tuxedo sings low and sincere,
While crickets do tap dance, they bring up the rear.

Fireflies twinkle, like tiny small stars,
They flash their secret code, 'Don't forget the jars!'
In this gentle twilight, with laughter unfurled,
Bright colors of humor paint over the world.

Touching the Soul with Violet

A sprinkle of mischief, a touch of delight,
The violet balloons float up into the night.
With giggles and snickers they rise up so high,
Saying 'Catch us if you can!' as they kiss the sky.

A cat with a bowtie invites all to dance,
While dogs in tutus join in on the chance.
With petals for confetti, the whole park will cheer,
In this touch of the soul, there's nothing to fear.

Essence of a Dreamy Dusk

In a world of purple hues,
I found a sock, not a shoe.
The moon laughed, bright and round,
As I tripped on dreams unbound.

Frogs croaked like a quirky band,
While fireflies danced, oh so grand.
I tried to catch one, oh what glee,
And woke up with a cheeky bee.

My pillow whispered tales so sweet,
Of fancy feasts and dancing feet.
But all I got was a sneezy cat,
Who played a tune, imagine that!

Under stars, I struck a pose,
To impress the flowers, I suppose.
They giggled softly, in delight,
As I tumbled in the fading light.

The Fragrance of Stillness

In the stillness of the night,
I saw a raccoon take a bite.
It stole my sandwich, what a thief,
With a sly grin, causing grief.

The daisies started a debate,
About the mint's unfriendly fate.
"I'm fresher!" cried a chipmunk near,
While I just stood, suppressing cheer.

A cricket chirped, a judge so grand,
As the flowers wobbled, hand in hand.
The moon chuckled at their plight,
While I snorted, what a sight!

A punchline spun beneath the stars,
As laughter echoed from the cars.
In the stillness, joy was found,
In silly moments all around.

Amethyst Elysium

In an amethyst garden of jest,
Where flowers giggle, oh what a fest!
A bumblebee wearing a tiny hat,
Danced with a snail, imagine that!

Petunias rolled their eyes in jest,
As daisies claimed to be the best.
"I can sing!" one tulip cried,
While I just laughed and nearly died.

A hedgehog in shades, quite the sight,
Sashayed smoothly in pastel light.
He slipped on a worm, what a blunder,
And the whole garden exploded with thunder!

As petals twirled in soft ballet,
I wondered how they'd end the play.
Their humor touched the heart in me,
In this wild amethyst spree.

Harmonies of the Lavender Sky

Under a sky of lavender hue,
A cat played piano, oh who knew?
He wore cute glasses, a sight to see,
As he belted out tunes, just for me.

The clouds joined in with a soft sway,
With rhythmical beats to light our day.
Each breeze carried a quirky tune,
As the sun danced with the lazy moon.

Frogs in bow ties formed a choir,
While ants waved flags in love's attire.
The chorus sang with all their might,
As I giggled aloud, what pure delight!

In this symphony of nature's song,
I felt like I could dance along.
With every note that drifted high,
I laughed beneath this lavender sky.

Blossoms in the Moonlight

In the garden where giggles grow,
Petals dance with the moon's soft glow.
Bumblebees buzzing in silly delight,
Tickling flowers, a comical sight.

Joking with shadows, they pirouette,
A sunflower spins, its hat's not yet.
Crickets join in with a laugh and a creak,
Tickling the night with their symphonic tweak.

The roses blush, they can't help but grin,
A daisies' joke? Oh, it's just a win!
Mice in tuxedos waltz without care,
While a frog in a top hat hums in midair.

Under stars, the garden's alive,
With silliness making the night thrive.
In this moonlit charm, we cannot forget,
Laughter blooms here; there's no need to fret.

Notes from a Lavender Heart

A heart that sings with purple tones,
Whispers funny lines in quirky tones.
It tickles the air with a silly rhyme,
Dancing through moments, making time shine.

With each chuckle, the petals sway,
Comedic chaos brightens the day.
A pun in the breeze makes laughter spring,
For even flowers enjoy a good fling.

The bees buzz tales of ridiculous dreams,
While hummingbirds practice their laugh-out-loud schemes.
A ticklish breeze rustles leaves and more,
As humor blooms at the garden's core.

In every petal, a joke does dwell,
A secret giggle, a funny spell.
With each note played from this cheerful heart,
Laughter's the tune; it's a whimsical art.

Serene Shades of Twilight

Twilight falls with a laugh so bright,
Colors giggle in the fading light.
Splashes of purple, a comical scene,
Where even the stars join in, so keen.

The clouds don hats, they're ready to play,
As shadows stretch out, they frolic away.
A giggling breeze fans the evening glow,
Strange little critters put on a show.

Whimsical dreams drift through the air,
Silly thoughts bounce without a care.
The fireflies wink with a cheeky grin,
As the night whispers where fun begins.

In this tranquil patch, silly winds blow,
A dance of laughter in twilight's flow.
With hues of mirth in the dusky sky,
Serene and funny, oh me, oh my!

Garden of Whispered Secrets

In a garden where secrets softly sigh,
Petals gossip as the breezes fly.
Butterflies chuckle, they can't keep still,
Each flit and flap brings a light-hearted thrill.

The herbs giggle, each leaf has a jest,
As the veggies grin, they feel quite blessed.
Tomatoes blush when the onions tease,
While carrots chuckle in the gentle breeze.

The daisies whisper tales of delight,
About a snail racing in jestful flight.
A hidden laugh echoes through the green,
In this playful garden, joy is seen.

Each secret shared brings a bounce to the day,
In a world of giggles, we dance and sway.
In this realm of whispers, humor beams,
Blooming with laughter, a garden of dreams.

Serenading the Night Bloom

In the garden where odd things thrive,
A cactus tried to dance, alive.
With petals swaying left and right,
But tripped on roots and lost the fight.

A buzzing bee joined in the fun,
Attempting moves, it overrun.
It rolled and tumbled, what a scene,
A comedy played, fit for a queen.

The moonlight chuckled, casting shade,
As flowers giggled, unafraid.
Their scent a mix of joy and jest,
In this floral show, they're truly blessed.

Yet all the while the nightingale,
Sang off-key in a fluffy veil.
A serenade of laughs, not tears,
Celebrating blooms with silly cheers.

Echoes of a Sunlit Past

In shadows of fond memories,
A daisy told jokes with such ease.
It spoke of days with laughter loud,
And hanging out with a funny crowd.

A sunbeam winked, quite bold and bright,
And made a squirrel lose its flight.
It chased its tail with dizzy spins,
As giggles echoed where warmth begins.

The daisies chuckled, leaning in,
"Remember when the sun fell in?"
They rolled in laughter, carefree, light,
Their petals bright against the night.

So here we share these sunny tales,
With humor woven through the trails.
When flowers laugh and time stands still,
Joy blooms eternal, a hearty thrill.

Soothing Shadows of Purple

In twilight's arms, a bobcat lurks,
Under lavender, it sneaks and smirks.
But stepping on a twig, oh dear!
The whole world knew that it was near.

It jumped and yowled, a sudden fright,
As petals swayed, a graceful sight.
With every thump and crash it made,
The flowers snickered in the shade.

A gentle breeze tossed scents around,
The giggles spun like merry sound.
In shadows soft, the night did play,
With funny sprigs that'd saved the day.

Each rustle held a secret laugh,
As nature painted joy's own path.
In soothing hues of purple light,
A comedy bloomed in the night.

Scented Hues of Serenity

There's fragrance in the air so sweet,
With flowers planning a prank complete.
A buttercup, all golden bold,
Wore a hat made of marigold.

"I'm the queen!" it proudly cried,
But the snickering blooms stood side by side.
With petals stirred by a playful breeze,
They laughed out loud with utmost ease.

The wind chimed in, a giggly friend,
Pushing blossoms as they bend.
They danced and twirled in joyful glee,
For innocence binds them, wild and free.

In colors bright, a tapestry spun,
Tickling senses, oh what fun!
So if you find a flower's joke,
Join the laughter, don't be broke.

The Tranquil Dance of Lavender

In fields so bright, they prance with glee,
Bouncing blooms, wild and free.
They tickle noses as they sway,
Whispers of purple laugh and play.

Buzzing bees join in the fun,
Unaware of the purple pun.
They sip and dance, a silly race,
From bloom to bloom, a honeyed chase.

A gentle breeze begins to tease,
Making flowers giggle with ease.
They shimmy left, then spin around,
In this purple place where joy is found.

With every sway, a joke is told,
In violet hues, the laughter's bold.
All nature's jesters, in a trance,
Stir up the air, let the flowers dance.

Rain on Purple Blooms

Upon the petals, the raindrops fall,
Tiny dancers, heed their call.
They slip and slide with a comic flair,
Watching flowers shake without a care.

The droplets giggle, as they glide,
Creating puddles where jokes abide.
The petals strain to hold their ground,
In a watery scene where laughter's found.

A clumsy bee slips, do a flip,
Landing right on a lilac ship.
The blooms erupt in a chuckling cheer,
As the rainy clown shows no fear.

In this playful storm, the colors gleam,
Purple hues, like a painter's dream.
With each splash, the joy takes flight,
In the garden's dance, oh what a sight!

A Canvas of Violet Reflections

Upon the canvas, colors blend,
Swirls of violet that never end.
With each stroke, a story spun,
Giggles trapped in the setting sun.

The painter's brush, a playful tease,
Looks for mischief in the breeze.
A splash of shade, a wink so sly,
As violet giggles glance the sky.

Drip-drip of paint from the brush's tip,
Creates a bloom with a comic quip.
The hues unite, both bold and bright,
In this garden, what a sight!

With laughter woven in every thread,
The flowers smile, where joy is spread.
Each petal's curve, a joke unspooled,
In violet joy, nature's ruled.

Soft Serenade of the Twilight Garden

As twilight whispers, the flowers hum,
A soft serenade, oh so fun.
The nightingale joins in delight,
Singing secrets in the purple light.

A bumblebee buzzes off-key,
Like a jester, can't you see?
The petals giggle, twirl about,
In this garden, laughter's out.

While fireflies dance, a glowing crew,
They twinkle jokes, just for you.
The night is young, with cheer so bright,
In the serenade of the starry night.

Each moment, a little comic bliss,
Nature's humor, impossible to miss.
Under a blanket of purple skies,
The garden laughs, oh, how it flies!

The Lullaby of Scented Breezes

In a field where the bees do dance,
The sneezing may leave you in a trance.
Dance around as the aromas play,
Chasing the butterflies all the way.

A breeze so sweet, it tickles your nose,
Watch out for pollen, that's how it goes.
With laughter that echoes through the tall grass,
You'll remember this day, oh, how it will last.

A picnic of puns, in a fragrant place,
Where even the ants join the funny race.
With giggles that bubble, just like the wine,
In this silly garden, everything's fine.

Oh, what a sight, to see your friends sneeze,
With tissue in hand, oh, how they tease.
A lullaby wrapped in petals so bright,
In the sweetest of scents, we find delight.

A Canvas of Violet Hush

A canvas spread wide with purple gleam,
The colors so vivid, you want to beam.
A painter who laughs with a brush in hand,
Accidentally spilled, oh what a grand stand!

Each stroke brings giggles, a blooper or two,
The ducks wear a crown—who knew it was blue?
With splashes of humor and whimsy's embrace,
This artful adventure is quite the fun case.

As a masterpiece grows in fits and in starts,
A thumbprint of chaos, oh, art has its parts!
With friends by your side, it's all just a game,
In the canvas of life, who's really to blame?

So dip into laughter, let colors collide,
In the hush of the violets, let go of your pride.
For each little mishap is a memory bright,
In the gallery of giggles, everything's right.

Echoed Melodies on Lavender Wind

A tune floats softly through the warm air,
It tickles your senses—a musical flair.
With hummingbirds laughing, they join in the fun,
Who knew that sweet songs could weigh just a ton?

The wind carries whispers, it seems to delight,
Each note a puff of a tickly bite.
Dance with the breezes, let worries take flight,
While the chorus of giggles keeps the mood light.

Oh, listen closely; do you hear the jest?
Socks on the grass! Is that really the best?
A melody made from the silliest sounds,
With each silly moment, pure joy knows no bounds.

In this whimsical concert, all creatures just sing,
From owls to old frogs, everyone's in swing.
With echoes that sparkle like stars up above,
Find humor in harmonies, laughter, and love.

Time Traveled Through Purple

Let's jump through the purple and into a scene,
With clocks that are melting, oh what does it mean?
A journey we take with giggles and grace,
In a time warp of joy, with silly hats in place.

Past moments of waltzes, turned lopsided too,
Dancing in circles, just me and you.
With every old joke, like a vintage fine wine,
We laugh until tears run, oh, it feels divine!

The past full of blunders, it gives us a thrill,
As we spin through the ages, our laughter will fill.
Each tick of the clock, brings a chuckle anew,
In this baffling timeline, all's funny and true.

So take my hand tightly, let's blink and explore,
Through the purple hues, we'll giggle for sure.
Where time's a mere jester, ever so spry,
In this endless delight, just you and I.

Essence of the Blushing Sky

In a field where bees do dance,
A flower winks, oh what a chance!
Twirling petals in the breeze,
Smells like snacks, oh what a tease!

The sun dips low, it starts to glow,
The flowers giggle, moving slow.
A daisy whispers, 'I adore!'
While sunflowers just beg for more!

A ladybug with spots like jam,
Sips the nectar, what a sham!
'Look at me, I'm quite the snack!'
As ants parade, they don't hold back!

In nature's jest, a silly show,
With scents so sweet, it's quite the glow.
The sky is blushing, can't deny,
In this garden, laughter's nigh!

Aromatic Echoes of Dusk

Whispers in the evening air,
Scented breezes, do they care?
Aroma dances, tickles the nose,
The evening blooms, in vibrant clothes.

Crickets chirp a funny tune,
While flowers sway beneath the moon.
The lavender giggles, lights a spark,
As shadows play, they fill the park.

A skunk waltzes, thinks he's suave,
'Fresh as a daisy', he tries to daub.
But friends just laugh, they tease and jest,
In this twilight, they're feeling blessed.

The stars above join in the fun,
While petals' laughter weighs a ton.
In nature's jest, here's the whisk,
Echoes float, it's quite the risk!

Reflections in a Purple Pond

A pond adorned with petals bright,
Frogs in shades of purple light.
They croak a song, each note a giggle,
While dragonflies just dance and wiggle.

Reflecting smiles on the water's face,
Tadpoles zoom, oh, what a race!
A turtle slow, his shell's a hat,
He waves hello, now that's quite fat!

The reeds are rustling, whispering tunes,
As fish bubble laughter, under the moon.
A duck slips by, and quacks a rhyme,
In this funny pond, we drift through time.

A splash, a dash, everyone's keen,
For silly moments, unseen, obscene.
Reflection laughs in every wave,
In this purple realm, we misbehave!

A Drift in the Violet Haze

In violet fog where breezes play,
A cloud of giggles leads the way.
A gopher twirls in dandelion fluff,
'Excuse my dance, but it's just enough!'

The air is sweet, a candy dream,
Puffballs float like whipped-up cream.
A squirrel jokes with a clever wink,
'Life's too short, let's laugh and drink!'

Butterflies in bright attire,
Flap their wings, inspire, inspire!
They play hopscotch on petals' tip,
While caterpillars take a trip.

In this haze where fun is king,
Nature's chorus begins to sing.
With every laugh, the world ignites,
In violet dreams, there are no fright nights!

Petals of Calm Reflection

In the garden, bees wear shades,
Tickled by flowers, in playful parades.
They buzz with jokes, a fluttering jest,
Nature's giggles put calm to the test.

The breeze plays tricks, like a sneaky cat,
Stealing a hat from a snoozing brat.
Petals are pillows for gnomes having naps,
While butterflies weave through whimsical traps.

Frogs croak rhymes, they're poets at heart,
Creating a symphony, a croaky art.
Leaves dance and blush at the silliest sight,
As sunlight giggles, painting the bright.

So let us prance where the gardens are wide,
With humor in bloom, join the merry ride.
Chasing our laughter, a picturesque spree,
In petal-clad meadows where joy likes to be.

Whispered Wishes in Violet Fields

In violet pastures, the wishes take flight,
Whispered by daisies, under moonlight.
Grasshoppers chuckle, with legs in a bind,
Creating a chorus that's goofy and blind.

The clouds wear hats, with styles that they flaunt,
While squirrels throw parties, a nutty jaunt.
One slips and tumbles, makes quite a scene,
And laughter erupts like a wild canteen.

Fields of delight, where the snickers abound,
Every whimsy without any ground.
Here laughter's the nectar, sweet and absurd,
And even the flowers can't help but be heard.

Join in the frolic, where wishes take root,
In a ticklish tapestry, life's just a hoot.
So let your heart giggle, and your spirit dance,
In whispered delight, take a silly chance.

Moonlit Perfume of Memory

The moon spills perfume, a scent of the past,
While raccoons in tuxedos hold parties unsurpassed.
They dance through the shadows, with mischief, they prance,
Creating a ruckus, a nocturnal dance.

Memory's tickles, spun with moonbeams,
Where laughter rolls in like wild-water streams.
A slip on the grass? Oh, what a delight!
Even stars chuckle at the frolic of night.

Fireflies flash jokes with their glowing rear ends,
As owls hoot laughter, the night never ends.
With each little twinkle, more giggles ignite,
In the fragrant embrace of this magical night.

So gather your joys, under starlit beams,
And dance through the whispers of sweet, silly dreams.
In this moonlit wonder, let your fun overflow,
With memories fragrant, in laughter we grow.

Shades of Serene Remembrance

In shades of serene, the memories play,
With laughter like ripples that dance on the bay.
A turtle dons glasses, pretending to read,
While fishes are gossiping, that's all they need.

Pastel-colored laughs float lazily by,
Balloons with wishes, catching a sigh.
A pig with a hat leads the troupe of delight,
As they glide through the clouds, soaring into the night.

The sun winks slyly, shedding rays of glee,
While crickets tell stories, as amusing as can be.
A tea party happens with daisies and more,
As creatures gather round, laughing in uproar.

So let us remember these shades of delight,
In moments that twinkle, and laughter shines bright.
With hues of the silly, we cherish and hold,
In serene recollections, our stories unfold.

Symphony of Calm and Color

In a garden, bees do hum,
With flowers dancing, oh what fun!
A spider spins its silky thread,
While ants march forth, their tales unsaid.

Butterflies wearing bows so bright,
They flutter round with pure delight.
With each petal, a giggle flies,
In this realm of calm, we laugh and sigh.

Whispers of Amethyst Dreams

A gnome once tried to plant a tree,
But tripped and fell—oh dear me!
His hat flew high, a grand display,
As squirrels laughed and ran away.

In moonlit nights, the shadowed prance,
A silly waltz, a clumsy dance.
They twirl in robes of deep, sweet hue,
As dreams creep forth, a cheeky view.

The Scent of Dusk's Embrace

The evening breeze begins to tease,
Whispers tickle through the trees.
A cat in shadows, spot on heart,
Takes the night as his own art.

While stars above throw cosmic plays,
A firefly winks in dim displays.
An owl hoots laughs with silly flair,
In dusk's embrace, we shed our care.

Fields of Purple Serenade

In fields aglow, the stories bloom,
Where bees do play and herbs consume.
A rabbit hops with no intent,
As daffodils cheer on, content.

The clouds above burst into song,
While crickets chirp along the throng.
A day of joy, a dance so free,
In purple fields, just you and me.

Dreamscapes in a Gentle Breeze

In fields where bees just sip and tease,
I danced with shadows under trees.
A butterfly with a fancy hat,
Said, 'What's the hurry? Let's have a chat!'

A wobbly worm in striped attire,
Told me a joke that sparked a fire.
We laughed so hard, the clouds turned pink,
And giggled bubbles began to stink!

With every breeze, a silly jig,
As daisies swayed, they'd dance a gig.
I lost my shoe, it flew away,
And landed on a goat that day!

So if you dream in colors bright,
With chuckles shared under moonlight,
Remember fields of greenish glee,
Where laughter grows like bumblebees.

The Air Thick with Purple Reverie

In a realm where socks don't match,
And gummy bears all watch the catch,
The sky was thick with fragrant glee,
As marshmallow clouds began to flee.

A dippy pixie flew so high,
With jellybeans and blueberry pie.
She tripped on clouds made out of fluff,
And giggled loud, 'This is just tough!'

An owl in glasses sipped his tea,
He winked at me, 'Now don't you see?
Life's but a jest, a comical race,
With rainbows dancing all over the place!'

Each laugh we shared was worth the fall,
So grab a friend, let's have a ball!
In dreams where purple whispers flow,
We'll ride on giggles, to and fro!

In the Heart of Violet Whispers

Beneath a sky of jelly blue,
A chubby cat with polka dots grew.
He spread his paws and took a leap,
Into a dream where we stink like sheep!

The dandelions wore a crown,
As squirrels danced in furry gowns.
A jester frog with a rubber shoe,
Declared, 'Come join, we've much to do!'

We twirled around, no care in sight,
While giggles echoed through the night.
With silly songs and rhymes absurd,
We painted tomorrows with each word.

So hold your hat, and take a ride,
On whims and giggles, side by side.
For in the heart where whimsy hides,
Lies laughter deep as ocean tides.

The Color of Stillness

In a world where stillness spins,
And chirping crickets wear their fins,
The quiet sang a tune so sweet,
As slippers danced on tiny feet.

A snail in shades of vibrant hue,
Said, 'Join my race, it's just for two!'
I chuckled loud, 'You'll win for sure,
With speed so slow, it's such a lure!'

The silence dripped like honey thick,
A playful breeze, a wobbly flick.
With colors soft and laughter near,
Life's quiet joy becomes so clear.

So take a breath and join the game,
Where stillness whispers without shame.
In this bizarre yet playful space,
We dance with smiles upon our face.

Whispers of the Purple Breeze

In a field where purple grows,
The bees play tag, and so it goes.
Butterflies dance, a waltz so spry,
They sip sweet nectar, oh my, oh my!

A squirrel wearing a tiny hat,
Chasing shadows—imagine that!
He slips and slides, a comical feat,
Then dusts off paws, feeling the heat!

The flowers giggle, their petals sway,
As birds crack jokes in a breezy play.
With buzzing buzz, and laughter loud,
Nature sings, a cheerful crowd!

Underneath the wide blue sky,
I think I heard a flower sigh.
"Let's prank the sun," they gleefully plot,
Till everyone joins—what a funny spot!

A Symphony in Lilac Hues

In a soft symphony of hues so bright,
The purple rain falls, oh what a sight!
A frog serenades with a skinny croak,
As flowers giggle at each tiny joke.

The wind hums tunes of tickling grass,
While squirrels rehearse their acorn class.
Chirping birds join the merry theme,
A wacky choir, a whimsical dream!

Butterflies flutter, with giggles uncurled,
A comical dance that twirls and swirled.
Petals prance, as if on a quest,
In this lilac world, there's never a rest!

As twilight whispers about the day,
A hedgehog tumbles in a fanciful way.
Nature chuckles, a hearty cheer,
In this violet bash, oh so dear!

The Scent of Evening Calm

As evening falls with a gentle sway,
A raccoon slips in to join the fray.
With mischief in mind, he plots his scheme,
To taste the scent of a flower's dream.

Cats chase shadows, tails held high,
While a snail claims he can surely fly!
The moonpeeking down, its glow so bright,
Winks at the antics, a joyful sight.

Breezes whisper secrets to the night,
"Who knew sweet flowers could be such a fright?"
They laugh in colors, a fragrant delight,
In the calm of evening, it feels just right!

A hedgehog's hat, a daisy crown,
As all join in without a frown.
The scent of fun in the air so warm,
In this charming garden, it's hard to conform!

Echoes of Violet Dreams

In violet dreams, the giggles rise,
As daisies wear their silly ties.
The sun rolls in like a laughing kid,
Promising fun with a wink, he hid.

The rabbits prance in shoes too big,
While the bumblebees dance a funky jig.
A butterfly trips on its own bright wings,
"What a blunder!" is how nature sings!

Clouds wear costumes, it's quite a show,
As shadows play tag, they dart to and fro.
With high-pitched laughs and skies so fair,
This playful land of purple flair!

In echoes of dreams, the night persists,
Where every flower has a funny twist.
Come join the fun, don't miss your chance,
In the garden of giggles, let's all dance!

The Color of Peaceful Days

A purple haze fills the air,
While bunnies hop without a care.
Sipping tea and eating pie,
I laugh as the butterflies fly.

The sun dresses in its finest hue,
Chasing shadows, oh so blue.
My hat's too big, it covers my face,
I trip on daisies, but it's all grace.

Clouds dance wildly across the sky,
I whisper secrets to a passing fly.
Chasing dreams on this day so bright,
Wishing each moment would take flight.

On peaceful days with skies so wide,
I wear my joys like a silly guide.
Laughter bubbles like a fish in a stream,
Oh, what a glorious, goofy dream!

Rhythm in the Bloom

In gardens where the giggles grow,
A funny rhyming worm steals the show.
He wiggles and squirms with such delight,
And dances around every flower in sight.

The bees gossip like little old ladies,
While snails groove like they're in the '80s.
I join the party with my own fine tune,
Twisting in circles under the moon.

With petals swaying in the breeze so free,
I tap my feet to their melody.
Nature chuckles as we all partake,
In this rhythm of joy, make no mistake!

Together we sway, the earth and I,
With every blossom, our spirits fly.
So here's to the laughter and silly songs,
In the bloom of joy, we all belong!

Petals on a Gentle Wind

Petals dance like clowns on parade,
A gentle wind gives them a swayed serenade.
I watch them twirl with a grin so wide,
As butterflies join in, full of pride.

A squirrel joins in, with quite the show,
Stashing acorns as they blow.
I laugh out loud at his frantic haste,
As petals swirl, oh, what a taste!

Every gust brings a new delight,
Like surprise parties in the daylight.
I catch a petal and wear it as a hat,
Feeling like royalty, imagine that!

With giggles carried on the breeze,
We joke with the trees, oh, what a tease!
Under the sky, with petals around,
We celebrate joy that knows no bound.

Memories of a Summer's Night

As fireflies twinkle like little stars,
I sip my drink from a jar with bars.
Laughter echoes through the warm, soft air,
While crickets play tunes without a care.

Marshmallows roast in a comedic plight,
One made a dive, oh what a sight!
We chuckle as the sticky hands abound,
In memories that dance all around.

The moon peeks in, a snicker or two,
While I tell tales of gooey fondue.
In every shadow, a funny face hides,
And joy rides the waves of nighttime tides.

In the warmth of the night, we sing and sway,
Cherishing moments, come what may.
With smiles and stories, laughter ignites,
In memories clad in summer's delights!

Essence of a Dusk Dream

In the garden where the gnomes play,
The flowers whisper jokes all day.
Bumblebees wearing tiny hats,
Dance to tunes of silly chats.

The sun dips low with a wink and grin,
As critters gather to join in.
Crickets' chirps are like a band,
While fireflies light up the land.

A fox wearing socks prances near,
Shouting, "Why drink water, I'll just steer?"
The world transforms, humor's here,
In this dusk where joy is clear.

Snapdragons pop with playful cheer,
As laughter flows from ear to ear.
In the dusk, dreams tumble and twirl,
Creating a whimsical, funny swirl.

Mood of the Lavender Skies

A cloud floats by, dressed in pink,
Whispering secrets, don't you think?
Squirrels gossip in goofy ways,
Making plans for nutty displays.

Rainbows slide down like slipping pies,
Filling the air with silly sighs.
Jokes on the wind, they swoop and swirl,
Even the trees begin to twirl.

A cat in shades lounges by day,
Sipping tea, he's here to play.
While robins sing tunes off-key,
In perfect harmony, can't you see?

With giggles echoing through the hush,
Even starlight begins to blush.
Under skies of artistic flair,
Life's just a canvas, bright and rare.

Soft Serenades of Nature's Palette

The daisies burst with laughter bright,
Tickling petals through day and night.
Bees engage in a wacky race,
Trying to keep up with the pace!

A bunny hops in polka-dot socks,
Crafting tunes while he rocks.
Grasshoppers join with jazz hands wide,
As daisies sway with blooming pride.

Chirping with joy, the sparrows sing,
Announcing that goofiness is king!
In the meadow, silliness grows,
With whispers of laughter, anything goes!

Nature's whispers become a cheer,
With every rustle, joy draws near.
In this palette, hues collide,
Painting smiles that can't be denied.

Amethyst Dreams at Dusk

Dusk drapes on with a velvet sigh,
As fruit bats zoom and swoop on by.
A gopher spins tales of heroics grand,
While fungi gather, part of the band.

Moonbeams laugh with a ticklish glow,
Sliding down trees for a nighttime show.
The owls pop popcorn, oh what a feat!
As a raccoon juggles for a treat.

Stars giggle in a twinkling spree,
Creating sketches from every tree.
With a spark, the night blooms bright,
Turning grumpiness into delight.

In this dream where silliness reigns,
Giggles ripple through the lanes.
Amethyst shades fill the air with cheer,
Making memories we hold dear.

A Song from the Enchanted Glade

In the glade where fairies prance,
Bouncing on their tiny feet,
They sing of jam and silly hats,
While dancing with a joyful beat.

A squirrel steals a cupcake here,
Giggles echo through the trees,
The gnome just spills his root beer,
And sneezes out confetti breeze.

The frogs join in with croaky laughs,
Trying to leap with all their might,
But end up in a sideway dance,
Underneath the moonlit night.

With chuckles shared among the crowd,
The butterflies spread dreamy cheer,
In the glade where joy is loud,
And laughter fills the atmosphere.

Night's Breath on Petals

With night's breath, the petals sway,
As crickets play their funny tune,
Bright fireflies join in the fray,
Dancing like a playful moon.

A cat tries to catch them all,
Then trips and lands in a pile,
The flowers giggle as they fall,
While moonlight shines with a smile.

A hedgehog joins the midnight show,
Bouncing on his little spine,
He rolls and tumbles with a glow,
Creating chaos, oh so fine!

The garden whispers tales of cheer,
As paws and wings make mischief brew,
In this night, we laugh and cheer,
For joy in quiet dreams we pursue.

Harmony in Shades of Indigo

In shades of blue, the jokes abound,
As indigo swirls in the breeze,
The flowers hum a silly sound,
Teasing bees who buzz with ease.

A wiggly worm in a top hat,
Twirls around, what a sight to see!
While daisies gossip, "How about that?"
"Is that worm really classy or free?"

A rabbit hops, oh can't you find,
A carrot shaped just like a shoe?
He places bets, "You won't unwind,
Bet you can't fit me, can you?"

The laughter echoes, hearts feel light,
In this patch where humor's grown,
We dance with joy, such sheer delight,
Finding silliness in the unknown.

Morsels of Memory in Bloom

In blooms of colors bright and bold,
Memory dances with delight,
Sharing stories that we've told,
As petals pirouette through the night.

A bee with an oversized hat,
Tries to sting a balloon, oh dear!
But ends up stuck, how about that?
Bouncing around, full of cheer!

The daisies shake their heads and say,
"What a day for sweet buffoonery!
Let's celebrate in our own way,
With a tea party among the tree!"

So here's to fun in flora's tongue,
With hearty laughs and stories spun,
In this garden where we belong,
Morsels of joy, forever sung.

Memories Wrapped in Purple

In fields where purple flowers sway,
I tripped on a bee, hey, what a day!
With laughter echoing near and far,
I wore a crown made of the bizarre.

Silly dances under sunny skies,
Caught my friend with a pie surprise.
We feasted well, with crumbs to spare,
And giggled 'til we gasped for air.

A petal tickled my funny bone,
Is it just me, or is that a cone?
Chasing dreams in that fragrant space,
Smiling wide, all thoughts erased.

So here's to quirks and silly schemes,
In shades of purple, we lived our dreams.
Gone are worries, let joy unfold,
In memories wrapped, forever bold.

Veils of Aromatic Dusk

As dusk drapes its fragrant veil,
I chased my cat, I must prevail!
Through scented shadow, there she goes,
In pursuit of a butterfly's toes!

The air is thick with stories sweet,
I slipped on grass and lost my feet.
My neighbor laughed, let's join the fun,
In our perfume game, we have won!

Her idea—let's make a big parade,
With mismatched hats, we've got it made!
We twirled and dipped under twinkling light,
Who knew that dusk would give such fright?

So here we are, with our rebel crew,
In veils of twilight, we start anew.
Laughter blooms in a purple haze,
Our aromatic dusk, a joke to praise!

Harmonies of the Violet Hour

At the violet hour, we sing and sway,
Jokes about socks with cakes on display.
With melodies drifting through the air,
We laugh at things that seem unfair.

A butterfly landed on my nose,
Its tickle made me strike a pose!
While friends record, we comb the breeze,
Sharing antics, aiming to please.

Suddenly, a tree mustered a grin,
I asked it where the laughter's been.
It creaked and cracked, what a gag,
Nature's humor in a plant's tag!

Together we blend, in our silly spree,
In harmony, wild and fancy-free.
So come join us, feel the power,
Of harmonies in the violet hour.

The Twilight Caress

In twilight's caress, we chase the light,
Dressed like ninjas, a comical sight.
With secret moves we skip and slide,
A giggling army, full of pride!

The moon peeks out, we hide behind trees,
While telling ghost tales that tease and please.
Each shadow flickers with laughter's sound,
With a leap and a shout, we're spellbound.

To prank our neighbors, we sneak and plot,
From grape juice mustaches, a silly spot!
With chaos and joy in the dampened grass,
We dance under stars that glimmer and pass.

So here's to the twilight, our playful friend,
In its gentle embrace, we laugh and ascend.
With each funny moment, we leave our mark,
In this twilight tale, igniting the spark!

Fields of Fragrant Serenity

In fields where scents do twirl and dance,
The bees all buzz in a silly trance.
A perfume wafts, oh what a tease,
While butterflies playtag in the breeze.

The sun shines bright, a golden glow,
As cows topple over, stealing the show.
We laugh at sheep with their curly q's,
Bahh! What's next? A cow that snooze?

With every whiff, a chuckle grows,
As friendly owls in sunglasses pose.
A goat in shades, oh what a sight,
Making fashion trends in daylight!

The air is filled with joy and cheer,
While squirrels dance, then disappear.
In fragrant fields, we skip and sway,
Giggling all the livelong day.

Twilight's Silken Veil

As twilight wraps the world in lace,
A raccoon joins the funny chase.
He lost his hat in the shadows' keep,
Through bushes, he dives—into a heap!

Firefly lights flicker, twirl, and zoom,
A beetle joins, drumming to the boom.
They argue loudly, who can flash bright?
But trip on wings and take off in fright!

Cicadas croon with a rhythm worn,
A chorus swells, and tune is born.
Karaoke night for creatures bold,
With crickets and frogs, the stage unfolds.

So here we laugh under the starry dome,
With whispers of nature, we find our home.
In twilight's glow, oh what a scene,
A fashion show for bugs, fit for a queen!

Caress of the Blossom's Breath

Petals flutter like jokes in the air,
As honeybees gather without a care.
They buzz and they bumble, oh what a team,
Competing for crowns in a sugary dream.

The flowers giggle, their colors collide,
A rainbow of humor, painting the wide.
Tulips in tutus, daisies in hats,
Playing charades with the chubby cats.

With each tiny breeze, a tickle ensues,
The grass blades are laughing, sharing their news.
"Did you hear the one 'bout a frog in a tree?"
"Jump on it, quick! Let's all see!"

A sunbeam shines with a beam of delight,
As blooms chuckle softly, inviting the night.
In the garden of giggles, our hearts find their rest,
With petals and laughter, nature's best jest.

Indigo Thoughts

In hues of deep blue, thoughts take flight,
Whimsical musings in the night.
A dolphin dons a silly cap,
While dreaming of donuts, perhaps a nap.

Stars wink down with mischievous glee,
A jester moon riding on a sea.
Fish in tuxedos swim with flair,
In a fancy ball, unaware of a bear.

Clouds puff and giggle, floating like dreams,
While rainbows play tag, bursting at seams.
A thoughtful owl in a chair made of glass,
Ponders the stars, and how they all dance.

So if you peek into the night sky,
And catch a star with a twinkle in eye,
Remember the laughter, let joy take its course,
In the indigo thoughts, let your spirit endorse!

Soft Murmurs of Spring's Kiss

The flowers giggle in the breeze,
As bees compete for tasty tease.
A butterfly does the cha-cha now,
While daisies cheer, "Oh wow, oh wow!"

The sun plays peek-a-boo in clouds,
As squirrels dance and gather crowds.
The tulips strut in colorful shoes,
And whisper secrets, sharing cues.

A bunny hops with style and flair,
Telling grass jokes without a care.
The daisies laugh 'til petals fall,
While giggling worms do stand-up tall.

So spring arrives with a silly grin,
In every nook, fun finds its kin.
With whimsy wrapped in joy so sweet,
We join the dance on happy feet.

Petal-Laden Daydreams

In the garden where sunflowers sway,
A cat nap's taken, 'til day turns gray.
Bees in tuxedos, buzzing just right,
Decide to throw a dance party tonight.

The daisies gossip, oh what a show,
As butterflies sail, to and fro.
A ladybug juggling, what a sight!
While ants all cheer—"You're outta sight!"

Clouds wear hats that spin and twirl,
As raindrops make a splashy swirl.
A snail races with a leaf like a sail,
While friends place bets—"To win, you'll fail!"

Petals rain down, like laughter's spread,
In a moment of joy, we're all well-bred.
Nature's quirks sing songs so dear,
In daydreams woven, let's all cheer!

The Lavender Heart of Twilight

Twilight whispers with a winking sun,
As crickets strum, the melody's fun.
A firefly flutters, wearing a hat,
While a turtle yawned, "Now that's where it's at!"

Stars start to giggle, one by one,
With dreams of marshmallows, oh what fun!
The moon joins in, a disco ball,
While tiny genies throw a gala ball.

The night blooms up with bright surprise,
As owls wear glasses and roll their eyes.
A raccoon peeks with a twinkle and grin,
"Can I show you how to dance? Come in!"

Time meanders in a comical way,
Leaving silliness to bright up the day.
With whispers of joy that never depart,
Under the twilight, a funny heart.

Notes from a Peaceful Realm

In a land where laughter grows on trees,
And rivers flow with fruity seas.
The clouds play drums with thunderous cheer,
While dancing moles put on a premiere.

A hedgehog strums a tune so bright,
As frogs croak beats under the moonlight.
The fish sing songs while swimming free,
Conducted by a starfish, quite a spree!

Flowers wear shades, sassy and bold,
While grasshoppers boast tales of old.
Each twig and leaf joins in the fun,
Exploding giggles 'til day is done.

Soft whispers echo through the air,
In this peaceful realm, we've nothing to spare.
So join the chorus, let laughter beam,
In this land of joy, we all dream!

Twilight's Fragrant Murmur

In a field where the bees do buzz,
A cow wears a hat, just because!
She dances and twirls in the sun,
While all of the flowers just run.

With petals that whisper and sigh,
A squirrel jokes, muttering 'Oh my!'
He steals a snack, then trips on a twig,
And tumbles down like a playful pig.

The sun dips low, twinkling bright,
The cat starts to chase a light.
The shadows twist, then grab a fight,
Yelling, 'Who's the funniest sight?'

As night arrives, the giggles spread,
Even mushrooms are laughing in bed.
The moon rolls out with a cheeky grin,
Promising chaos, let the fun begin!

Hues of Tranquil Twilight

The sky paints jokes with a brush,
While owls giggle and woodland creatures hush.
A raccoon tips his hat, quite grand,
As fireflies waltz, light up the land.

The breeze carries whispers and pranks,
A spider spins doodles, earning thanks.
A chicken joins in the evening fun,
Clucking a tune, under the sun.

Colors swirl, as the stars appear,
The clouds drift by, dodging all fear.
A frog on a lily, croaks his dear song,
While the pond reflects that he's not wrong.

The night unfolds with magic and zest,
In every nook, there's humor expressed.
As laughter echoes through fields and trees,
The shades of twilight bring tales and glee!

Aroma of the Evening Sky

With scents so sweet, the air is alive,
A skunk in a tuxedo, ready to strive.
He dances a jig, quite out of tune,
While crickets just laugh at his funky croon.

The lilacs are gossiping low and loud,
Making fun of a passing cloud.
They giggle, they snicker, they just can't stop,
As bees all buzz in a comical hop.

The dusk does unfold a whimsical sight,
A hare dons a cap, joining the night.
He gives a salute to the stars above,
And winks at the world with a chuckle of love.

With ripples of joy, the twilight plays,
In jokes and aromas, it sweetly sways.
Each breeze carries laughter, quite spry,
In this fragrant evening, we all just fly!

Violet Echoes in the Breeze

In a garden of giggles, colors collide,
A gopher sneezes, with flowery pride.
The daisies all chuckle and sway with glee,
As the wind passes through, a ticklish spree.

The dusk brings a party, laughter so bright,
Crickets in bow ties throwing a light.
A hedgehog rolls in a party of blooms,
Cheering on friends in the peaceful rooms.

As shadows stretch, the moon starts to glow,
Fireflies dance, and the night puts on a show.
A comical frog sings a ditty so high,
While the stars gather 'round, waving goodbye.

With echoes of violet drifting away,
Every critter joins in and starts to play.
In this whimsical world, where chuckles reside,
The breeze carries joy like a merry ride!

Nightfall's Gentle Pastels

In the garden, dusk begins to play,
Bumblebees tiptoe, they're here to stay.
A cat in a bowtie, struts with flair,
Chasing shadows, without a care.

Stars giggle as they peek through the trees,
An owl hoots softly, "Hey, where's my cheese?"
The stars wink back, their tiny lights blink,
And the moon scribbles jokes in pink.

Fireflies dance in a zany parade,
While raccoons debate on plans they made.
The breeze lets out a chuckle, it seems,
Whispering secrets of nighttime dreams.

As nightfall wraps us in soft amends,
Funny whispers tell of playful trends.
In pastels of laughter, we play along,
This night's a giggle—a whimsical song.

Whispering Fields of Dream

In fields where the whispers choose to go,
Silly dreams bounce high and low.
A sheep in pajamas counts with flair,
Tickling daisies without a care.

Clouds stretch like cats in a sunny embrace,
A butterfly races, a comical chase.
Worms share a joke while they dig and squirm,
While flowers nod, "Life's a splendid term!"

The wind plays tricks, lifts hats to the sky,
While the sun and moon wink, and pass by.
Crickets croon tales in the chirpiest tone,
Making melodies fit for a throne.

In this field of giggles, we laugh and shout,
Chasing wonder, there's never a doubt.
With whispers of joy in our silly scheme,
Together we frolic—oh, what a dream!

The Silent Song of Purple

In a quiet grove where purple sprawls,
A gopher tap dances, while everyone calls.
With a top hat sleek and a cane of a twig,
He pirouettes nimbly, oh what a gig!

Bonnets too tight on buzzing bees' backs,
They hum to the rhythm of picnic snacks.
A gnome with a wink shares a chuckle or two,
As tulips gossip about morning dew.

Socks on the grass, mismatched with pride,
Little hampsters take a joyous ride.
Frogs in tuxedos, croaking a tune,
Inviting all guests to a grand balloon.

With whispers of laughter, let's dance and sway,
In this purple realm, come join the fray.
The silent song of joy is quite clear,
So let's clap our hands and cheer without fear!

Twilight's Aromatic Dreamscape

In twilight's glow, the aromas arise,
Skunks in sunglasses, oh what a surprise!
A hedgehog in rollerskates zooms right past,
While the moon plays fetch with the stars upcast.

Whiffs of sweet nonsense fill up the air,
A cabbage in ribbons caresses a chair.
The twilight giggles, "What nonsense we weave!"
While frogs in tuxedos start to conceive.

A parade of oddities marches about,
With spoons and forks chanting a lively shout.
The cauldron of dreams bubbles over with cheek,
As crickets recite the silliest week.

In this aromatic scene, we twirl and swing,
With laughter that drips from everything.
Join in the fun, let the twilight delight,
In this dreamscape, we dance through the night!

Essence of Gentle Reverie

In a field of whispers, bees do sway,
They sing of honey, and then fly away.
A breeze so light, it tickles the nose,
Yet here I am, tangled in my clothes.

Clouds roll by, like cakes on a plate,
With icing so sweet, I challenge fate.
But oh, the ants, in formation they march,
They steal my crumbs beneath the sun's arch.

Giggles erupt from a nearby tree,
A squirrel in shorts is a sight to see.
I'm sipping tea, watching nature play,
In a silly dream that won't go away.

So dance with the daisies, take a spin,
They wink and twirl, let the laughter begin.
In the heart of this whimsy, joy is found,
With a sprinkle of petals swirling 'round.

In the Embrace of Purple Shadows

Beneath a sky painted in violet hues,
I trip on my laces, and oh, what a ruse!
A butterfly giggles as it does a loop,
While I make a face, feeling like a stoop.

Wobbly sunflowers lean in to chat,
They claim I'm the clumsiest of all the fat.
With roots in the ground, they're here to stay,
While I take a tumble and roll away.

Jesters of nature, with petals so bright,
Tease me with laughter, oh what a sight!
The grass is a carpet where mischief is brewed,
Every step forward throws me heartily skewed.

So I'll join their party, let the frolic unfold,
With giggling daisies, both daring and bold.
In purple shadows, I dance with delight,
For laughter's the magic that makes it all right.

The Melody of Floral Calm

A bloom in the garden strikes a funny pose,
It sways and jiggles, does a toe-to-toe.
While bees buzz in rhythm, trying to hum,
I'm caught breathing in, what of this is dumb?

The roses declare, "We're royalty here!"
While tulips shout, "Don't pull on my ear!"
A marigold mocks with a cheeky grin,
As I thrift in the chaos, a wild spin win.

The daisies are gossiping, spilling the tea,
On who stole the sunshine from next to the bee.
While I pluck a pansy, it grumbles in jest,
"Just look at the fool who's always so stressed!"

In this floral ballad, where laughter ignites,
The petals are singing with sheer delight.
Join in with a chuckle, under sun's balm,
For the world's a stage, in this melody calm.

Murmurs of a Distant Shore

Waves tickle the sand in a bubbly approach,
Seagulls squawk loudly, a raucous reproach.
Shells laughing softly, tell secrets to me,
Of mermaids who lost all their dignity.

A crab in a tuxedo, all dapper and grand,
Seeks a dance partner, but runs from my hand.
The seaweed does shimmy, a green little sway,
While I offer the crabs my own ballet.

A dolphin with shades laughs at my style,
As I tumble and roll, gaining sand's great mile.
The waves tease me kindly, "Come join the parade!"
Oh, how I love this aquatic charade!

So let's skip on the shoreline, all silly and free,
With water and laughter, just you and me.
In murmurs of joy, nature plays her score,
As we frolic together by the ocean's roar.

Enchanted Nights of Scent

Under the stars, the aroma flows,
A curious blend, who really knows?
The moon giggles, its light a tease,
While critters dance, doing as they please.

A fairy sneeze sends sprigs in flight,
The flowers laugh, what a silly sight!
Bumblebees buzz with a jolly hum,
In this wild night, we all feel young.

The breeze carries tales from lands afar,
With every whiff, we smell a bizarre.
Invisible socks that tickle our toes,
Join us tonight, where the fun just grows!

So sip your tea, and share a jest,
In the garden's glow, we truly are blessed.
With laughter so rich, and dreams taken high,
Who knew the night could be this spry?

The Calm in Shades of Violet

In shades of purple, we find our peace,
With hues so calm, our worries cease.
A snail in a bowtie takes a slow stroll,
While crickets compose their night-time roll.

The flowers gossip, it's quite absurd,
A bee misheard a fanciful word.
A butterfly flits with an elegant grace,
Tripping on petals, it loses face!

Old twigs perform a humorous dance,
As nature's stage takes a wild chance.
With every giggle, the stars pay heed,
To frolicsome nights where silliness leads.

So let's hold hands, in this hue divine,
And make up stories with sweet punchlines.
For in shades of violet, we'll surely find,
A laughter that echoes, one of a kind!

Misty Meadows of Memory

In misty meadows, laughter rings clear,
With whispers and echoes for all who hear.
A squirrel in boots spins tales of old,
While shadows of memories break from the cold.

The daisies chuckle, teasing the breeze,
With hints of mischief, they do as they please.
A rabbit recounts his clumsy dance,
While clouds join in with a puffy prance.

In this place of whimsy, we dream awake,
As petals tickle, and soft branches shake.
We trip on the sunbeams that sprinkle the ground,
Creating remembered moments all around.

So gather the giggles and keep them near,
In misty meadows, we conquer our fear.
With every memory that makes us smile,
We'll cherish this fun, all the while!

Lullabies in Lavender Fields

Lullabies drift through fields of delight,
Where flowers sway in the quiet night.
The worms hum a tune, quite off-key,
As crickets hold concerts, feeling quite free.

A goat in a hat joins the soft croon,
While fireflies dance like sparks of moon.
With melodies flowing, we sway and spin,
Who knew that laughter could bubble within?

The clouds yawn wide, sharing soft dreams,
As the sun peeks over, in golden beams.
With giggles and sighs, we drift on the breeze,
To a place where humor brings hearts to ease.

So hum those tune, let your troubles go,
In lavender fields, love's laughter will grow.
With every note sung, we find our way,
To whimsical nights that brighten our day!

www.ingramcontent.com/pod-product-compliance
Lightning Source LLC
Chambersburg PA
CBHW071828160426
43209CB00003B/238